EUROPEAN REGULATION OF ADVERTISING